—THE GREAT BOOK OF—

ANIMALS

RAY ROURKE PUBLISHING COMPANY, INC
WINDERMERE, FLORIDA 32786

Library of Congress Cataloging in Publication Data

Taylor, Ron (Ron B.)
   The great book of animals.

   Includes index.
   SUMMARY: Discusses the lives of wild animals,
how they adapt to different environments, how they
hunt their prey, and how they defend themselves
from attack.
   1. Animals — Juvenile literature.   [1. Animals]
QL49.T24   1981   591   81-12032
ISBN 0-86592-065-6   AACR2

**Right: This lizard from Australia
displays its frill to make itself look
fiercer.
Previous pages: A cheetah, the fastest
land animal, at top speed.**

**COVER: A mandrill, a colorful
baboon. Top of box: A chameleon changes
colour to match its surroundings; polar
bears. Centre of box: A tiger on the prowl
in Asia. Bottom of box: Prairie dogs
burrowing underground; a Canadian lynx,
a member of the cat family.**

-THE GREAT BOOK OF-
ANIMALS

RAY ROURKE PUBLISHING COMPANY, INC
WINDERMERE, FLORIDA 32786

Contents

Editorial

Author Ron Taylor

Designer Keith Groom

Editor Angela Royston

Published by Ray Rourke Publishing Company, Inc.
Windermere, Florida 32786.
Copyright © 1981 Grisewood & Dempsey, Ltd.
Copyright © 1981 Ray Rourke Publishing Company, Inc.

Animals

Most cities have a large well-stocked zoo. Lively monkeys, dignified lions and tigers, hugely impressive elephants and rhinos are among the most popular attractions. No wild place has such a wide variety of wild animals. Yet animals in the wild, although they are often difficult to find, are more interesting because they behave more naturally.

Animals are suited to the kind of places, or environments, they live in. A camel is well equipped to survive in the desert, a polar bear in the Arctic. The first part of this book introduces different environments and some of the animals that live in them.

We find some animals more attractive than others: furry koala bears, for example, are more endearing than venomous snakes. But life in the wild can be fierce and competitive. All animals have to eat to live. Some eat only plants. Others eat meat, and must prey on other animals. The last part of the book looks at how animals hunt their prey and defend themselves from attack.

An African elephant

Forest Animals

Woods and forests are full of life. Of course, the forests themselves *are* life — large trees, bushes, creepers and undergrowth plants. All this plant life provides plenty of food for animals.

The tropical rain forests of Africa, South America and Malaysia contain the greatest variety. Many thousands of animal species live in these great, steamy expanses of jungle. Rain-forest animals include the jaguar, which is a particular kind of large cat, as well as many kinds of colorful birds, apes and monkeys, and a multitude of snakes and insects.

Different sorts of animals live in the cooler forests away from the Tropics. Badgers, bears

◄ The orangutan lives in the steamier rain forests of southeast Asia. It uses its long arms and gripping hands and feet to swing from tree to tree.

▼ Brown bears from the pine forests of North America and Russia often catch fish from forest streams and rivers.

# of Life

and squirrels live in temperate forests, together with wood pigeons, woodpeckers and many other birds.

Although a forest may contain many animals, you could walk in one for an hour or more without noticing a single living creature, other than, perhaps, a bird or an insect. Forest animals are expert at concealing themselves among the leaves or undergrowth, either to escape from their enemies, or in readiness to pounce on an unsuspecting victim. For example, a chital deer is well concealed by its spotted coat among the undergrowth of its native Indian jungles, but its enemy the tiger is also well hidden by its stripes.

▼ These birds of paradise come from the jungles of New Guinea and Australia, where the dense foliage hides their brilliant colors.

Most forest animals, such as this fruit-eating turaco from Africa, are the same color as the trees they live in. ▼

Desert Animals

◀ The Gila monster is a lizard that lives in desert country in the southern USA and northern Mexico. It is called a monster because it is one of the only two venomous lizards. The other is the beaded lizard which looks rather similar. These are slow-moving lizards, which use their poison to slow down and kill their speedier prey.

▶ For most snakes moving through the loose desert sand would be a problem. This rattlesnake manages because it has evolved a peculiar method of moving called sidewinding. Only two points on the under-side of the snake's body touch the sand at any one time. This gives the snake a better purchase or hold on the slippery sand. It also prevents the snake's body becoming over-heated from too much contact with the hot sand.

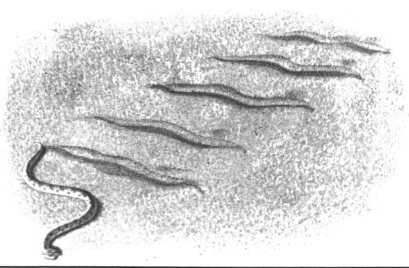

Deserts are generally very hot in the daytime but can be quite chilly at night. As this desert lizard warms up in the morning sun, it becomes more active.

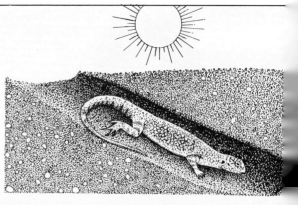

When the sun gets too hot for the lizard's comfort, it seeks the cool of its burrow. There, it sleeps during the heat of the day, until the sun begins to set.

▶ The camel is well suited to desert life. Its feet splay out to bear its weight on the soft sand. Its long eyelashes keep fine sand out of its eyes. Its hump is a food store for long journeys.

If forests are crowded with animal life, then deserts, you might think, are empty of it. This is not so. Desert animals are not as numerous as forest animals but they are widespread and varied, and form thriving animal communities.

Most desert animals are small, although one or two such as the camel are large. All desert animals have evolved special ways of surviving in the hot, arid wastelands. Smaller desert animals often avoid the fierce heat of the daytime sun by burrowing underground or sheltering under stones. At night the desert comes to life as its animal inhabitants wake up and creep out from their holes and sheltering places.

Since plant life is so scarce, many animals are hunters, if only on a small scale. Desert foxes and snakes may like the taste of a fat gerbil or other desert rodent, but they may often have to be content with a few insects. The gerbil itself lives on stores of plant food – for even the desert blooms from time to time when it rains.

Then, the lizard comes out once more to feed. But the desert sands are still hot from the sun, so the lizard climbs onto a desert plant until the sand has cooled down.

The fennec is a little desert fox with very big ears. It uses them not only for listening out for its prey and for its enemies, but also for keeping cool in the hot desert climate. Big ears lose more heat than small ears. An Arctic fox has very small ears (see page 17), while a common red fox has medium-sized ears.

Plains Animals

Different countries have different sorts of plains, or large areas of flat land. In countries with cool or temperate climates and many rivers, the plains are usually green and fertile. In hotter countries with fewer rivers and lakes, plains are barer of grass and browner in color. Sometimes they merge at their edges into dry, arid areas of scrub.

Populations of wild animals vary with the type of plains on which they live. The plains of northern Europe with their juicy grass

▼ Prairie dogs are not dogs but relatives of squirrels. They live in burrows on the North American plains.

▼ **This family of lions, and the elephants, antelope and ostriches in the background, live on the hot grassy plains, or savannah, of Africa.**

are mainly grazed by domestic cattle and sheep, but wild animals such as rabbits and field mice live there too.

The grasslands of Africa look less lush, but are the home of many of the world's large animals. The coarse grass and small bushes provide food for large herds of zebras, antelopes and wildebeest. Smaller groups of giraffes and elephants feed on the leaves of trees, while buffaloes and rhinos crop the grass. Lions are their largest enemies and await their chance to outrun and hunt down the weak or unwary.

The grasslands of several other countries are also hot and dry, but very different kinds of animals live on them, such as armadillos and giant anteaters in South America, and kangaroos, dingoes and rabbits in Australia.

▼ **African rhinos are also savannah animals. This white rhino has a broad, flat mouth suitable for cropping grass close to the ground.**

Mountain Animals

◀ An ibex eats almost any kind of plant food, and so can live high in the mountains even during winter, when the grass may be buried under snow.

▼ The mountain goat (left) and the chamois (right) are true mountain dwellers, confident and secure on the highest rock or narrowest ledge.

For an animal, mountain life has its advantages and its disadvantages. On the one hand, a true mountain animal, such as a chamois or other type of mountain goat, is safe from most enemies on its high crags. A smaller mountain animal, such as a marmot (very like the prairie dogs on the previous page) or a pika, can hide safely from attack among the many rocks and hollows of its mountain home.

On the other hand, high mountains are very harsh and inhospitable places, especially through their long, bitterly cold winters, when plant food is very scarce and

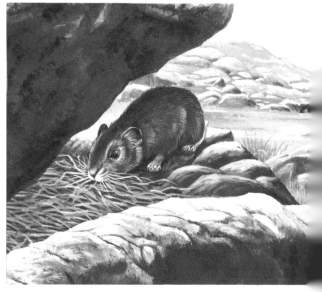

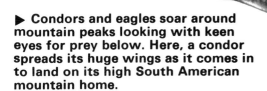

► Condors and eagles soar around mountain peaks looking with keen eyes for prey below. Here, a condor spreads its huge wings as it comes in to land on its high South American mountain home.

Pikas are close relatives of rabbits and hares. Many pikas live in cold, mountainous areas, where they feed by grazing the sparse cover of greenery, hiding behind the rocks from their enemies.

may be buried under thick snow. For this reason many mountain animals, including brown bears and mountain squirrels, hibernate or sleep through much of the winter, waking only at long intervals to forage for food.

An animal that lives on the steepest, rockiest parts of mountainsides has to be very sure-footed if it is not to fall and injure itself. A mountain goat is able to make dizzy leaps from crags to ledges and back again because its cloven hoofs have a very sure grip on the rockface. In winter the mountain goat is kept warm by its dense hairy coat. Also, like other kinds of goats, it is able to live off almost any kind of plant food.

Mountain birds have to contend with strong upcurrents and gales. Many small birds hop around in search of insects and seeds, but larger hawks and eagles are strong enough to use the upcurrents to soar among the mountain peaks. They have remarkable eyesight and swoop down to pick up rabbits, mice and smaller birds far below. Beetles, flies and mites can also survive mountain life, living on food such as pollen.

Life in the Cold

There is almost nowhere on the face of the Earth where animals do not live. Even deserts support animals which can withstand heat and drought.

The freezing wastelands of the polar regions are just as uninviting as the waterless deserts, but for different reasons. Here there is no shortage of fresh water. It is all around as snow and ice. But green plants, which provide so many animals with their food, are absent or rare in the white expanses of the Arctic and Antarctic regions. Only in the few weeks of summer do they grow at all, and then only around the fringes of these cold lands.

Life in polar regions depends on the sea. The freezing polar waters are very rich in plant life, the floating plankton. Plankton contains uncountable billions of tiny green plants and equally small animal life which feeds on these plants. In turn, these small animals are food for larger animals including the largest animals of all, the great baleen whales, which feed only on small shrimp-like krill.

Other large polar animals depend less directly on plankton. The polar bear kills seals for its food; the leopard seal skins and eats penguins. Other seals, and penguins, live on fishes. But all these animals depend, ultimately, on the plankton.

The Emperor penguin hatches its eggs by holding them off the snowy ground with its feet, keeping them warm against its body. When the eggs hatch, the penguin chicks are kept warm in the same way.

Small Life in the Arctic

Insects and other very small creatures depend largely on plant life, particularly flowers. When winter comes, most insects die off with the cold. So you might suppose that no insects live in the Arctic, a land of almost perpetual ice and snow. In fact, almost the opposite is true. During the short Arctic summer, when thick carpets of flowers spring up to cover very large areas, butterflies, flies, bees and other winged creatures can be seen feeding from the flowers. Arctic insects can produce such vast swarms that they become a plague both to Arctic animals and to the Eskimo and Lapp peoples. Great herds of caribou—first cousins of reindeer—roam the Canadian Arctic. In summer, the midges and mosquitoes pester them so much that they prefer to keep to the snow-covered areas where food is more scarce, rather than travel where food is plentiful but where the biting insects perpetually swarm.

A scene on the ice floes of the Arctic ocean. A polar bear (1) tends her young cubs, which she will later teach to hunt fishes and other small prey. When they are fully grown they will be able to kill large seals like the one shown slipping into the water (2). In the background gallops a short-eared Arctic fox (3), perhaps in pursuit of an Arctic bird such as the razorbill (4) sitting on the right. The birds flying overhead are little auks (5), the smallest diving sea birds. This is a very crowded scene for the Arctic, where on most days you would be lucky to see even one of these animals.

◄ These belugas, or white whales, are larger relatives of porpoises and dolphins. They live in the freezing cold seas of the southern Arctic, in herds or families, and hunt fishes for food.

Comparing

Fish Facts

The largest fish in the world is the whale shark, shown on the right. This great spotted monster grows up to 66 feet (20 meters) long and can weigh 70 tons—the weight of nine large elephants. Only the giant sea mammals, the great whales, are bigger than the whale shark. By contrast, the smallest of all fishes is probably the Luzon goby of the streams of Southeast Asia. This is less than 0·5 inches (just over a centimeter) long when fully grown.

Record Rodents

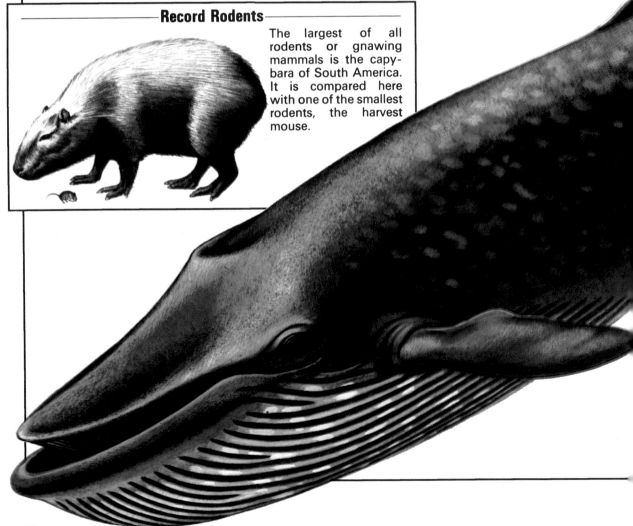

The largest of all rodents or gnawing mammals is the capybara of South America. It is compared here with one of the smallest rodents, the harvest mouse.

Animals

Biggest and Heaviest

Largest of All

The blue whale is the largest animal that has ever lived. It grows to over 98 feet (30 meters) long and weighs up to 140 tons—as much as 18 large elephants.

Giraffe
18 feet (5·5 meters) high—tallest land animal.

Elephant
11·5 feet (3·5 meters) high; weighs over 6 tons—heaviest land animal.

Reptile Records

● The biggest reptiles are salt-water crocodiles, which can be up to 20 feet (6 meters) long but are much thicker-bodied than snakes.

● Longest of all snakes is the anaconda of South America (right). It is the biggest of the boa family, thick-bodied snakes which crush their prey to death before swallowing it whole. Anacondas grow up to 33 feet (10 meters) or more long. The smallest snakes only grow up to 4 inches (10 cm) long.

Bird Facts

By far the largest of all living birds is the ostrich of the African plains. It stands nearly 8 feet (2½ meters) high and can weigh 308 lb (140 kilograms). Smaller, but still very large, flightless birds are the emu of Australia, the cassowary of New Guinea forests, and the rhea of South America. The smallest bird is the bee hummingbird from Cuba. It is only 2 inches (5 cm) long and weighs about 0·1 ounces (2·8 grams). The smallest European bird is the goldcrest at 0·5 ounces (14 grams).

Fastest Movers

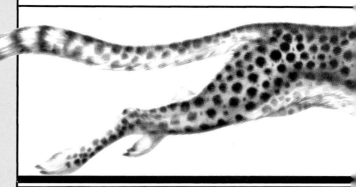

● Fastest land animal is the cheetah, which has been known to achieve a speed of 84 mph (135 kph)—faster than most motorists are allowed to go.

● Even speedier movers are some birds, notably the spine-tailed swift, which probably can dive at more than 186 mph (300 kph) and more usually flies at speeds over 87 mph (140 kph).

● The fastest snake is the black mamba, which is also one of the deadliest. However, as a fast mover perhaps it is a bit of a disappointment, because despite rumors of its being able to catch up with and attack a running man, it probably cannot travel at more than 7 mph (11 kph).

● The fastest creature in the oceans is the swordfish, which, surging through the surface layers in pursuit of its flying fish prey, can reach more than 56 mph (90 kph).

● But for their size, some insects are also very fast movers. A bee moves through the air at speeds up to 14 mph (22 kph), and a dragonfly can zip along at speeds up to 20 mph (32 kph). Insect wings beat at a tremendous rate—as many as 57,000 beats per minute.

Long Jumpers

Most famous of jumping animals are the kangaroos. A large kangaroo was once seen to make a jump of nearly 43 feet (13 meters). For its size, the tiny flea can make even more remarkable jumps, reaching as much as 10 inches (25 cm) in height, or 12 inches (30 cm) in length—about 200 to 300 times its own body length. Frogs, also famous jumpers, have been known to leap more than 16 feet (5 meters), or about 30 times their own length.

The white stork is a large bird that migrates from Europe to South Africa. It can only cross the sea at narrow channels.

The Arctic tern is the champion of all migratory birds, flying 10,000 miles (16,000 kilometers) between the polar regions.

The bobolink is a song bird which migrates between its breeding grounds in the north of Canada and the south of Argentina.

▶ The peregrine falcon is one of the fastest moving birds as it dives at 290 kph (180 mph), but the swift is even faster.

◀ The cheetah at full stretch is the fastest of all land animals.

Fastest and Farthest

Many animals need to be able to move very quickly. They include hunters chasing their prey, and prey escaping hunters. The cheetah, fastest of all land animals, is a hunter which attacks with a tremendous burst of speed, but gives up if it does not catch its prey within the first few minutes.

Other animals are capable of more sustained effort. Birds will often make migrations over vast distances, sometimes without seeming to take any rest. Social insects such as ants, bees and wasps seem to be incessantly on the move, at least during the warm months of the year.

Long-distance Travelers

Many animals make migrations, or regular long-distance journeys from one place to another. They may be seeking the sun, as with the swallows that leave the shores of Europe in early autumn for the warmer ones of Africa. Or, like the caribou of Canada, they may make long journeys in search of food. Yet other animals migrate to faraway places to breed. The most famous example is the common eel, millions of which migrate every year from North America and right across the Atlantic from their native European rivers to their spawning ground in the Sargasso Sea. Champion of all migrators, however, is the Arctic tern, a small bird that migrates the immense distance from the Arctic to the Antarctic and back every year.

Monarch butterflies migrate in enormous swarms from Canada to Mexico. Some of them drift out over the Pacific Ocean.

The common eel migrates thousands of miles from N. American and European rivers to spawn in the Sargasso Sea. The young eels return to the same rivers.

Strange Animals

Many animals seem strange to us simply because we see them only very rarely, so they come as a great surprise to us when we do encounter them—usually at the zoo.

Some animals, though, really do live very strange lives. For example, the vampire bat shown in the photo lives entirely on blood, a way of life bizarre enough to have given rise to the Dracula legend.

Some animals are strange because they appear to be mixtures of other animals. The most famous example is the platypus shown below. This is really a primitive sort of warm-blooded mammal but it has many of the features of a cold-blooded reptile.

Even animals which are more or less familiar to us may have odd features to their lives. Most people know what a kangaroo looks like, but very few have seen a newborn kangaroo, which is very tiny, blind and hairless. Despite its apparent helplessness —it is only about half an inch (a centimeter) long—a newborn kangaroo finds it own way to its mother's pouch.

Australian Oddities

◀ Koalas eat only eucalyptus leaves. This koala snoozes peacefully in its home tree. It spends the first six months of its life in its mother's pouch, the next six clinging to her back.

▶ A young kangaroo, or joey, sucks milk from the teat inside its mother's pouch.

◀ The platypus is a very strange animal. It has a flat tail and webbed feet like a beaver, but a horny bill like a duck. It has hair like a mammal, yet it lays eggs like a reptile. Also like a mammal, it feeds its young on milk—but the milk oozes out of slits, not teats as in other mammals.

▼ The pangolin, shown
stretched out on a branch
and also curled up asleep, is
another eater of ants and
termites. Unlike all other
mammals, its body is covered
by large scales, so that it
looks rather like a long,
active pine cone!

▲ Most bats eat insects, but this vampire bat
drinks only blood. In its tropical American home,
a vampire sucks blood from larger animals and
people, but this captive bat sips its blood from
a bottle-top. This strange-looking creature was
the inspiration for the fictional character
Count Dracula, who lived on human blood and
turned his victims into vampires too.

The axolotl nor-
mally never grows
into an adult. It
is a giant tadpole
which lives in
water all its life,
breathing through
gills. In captivity,
however, it can
be made to lose
its gills and turn
into a land-living
salamander.

▶ The aardvark is a
South African animal
that lives on termites.
It digs these little
creatures out from
their hard-walled
nests with its
tremendously
strong claws, and
licks thousands
of them up
with its long
thin tongue.

▲ The North American buffalo or bison was hunted almost to extinction in the last century.

▲ American alligators were once hunted for their hide. Now, they are being killed off by water pollution.

▼ The sea otter was almost wiped out for its beautiful fur. It is now protected.

▲ The Californian condor, largest American bird of prey, has been hunted nearly to extinction.

▲ The rock fowl lives in West African forests. But these are rapidly being felled.

▼ The Caspian tiger was once common in the northern forests of Iran but may now be completely extinct in the wild.

▲ The Spanish lynx is fast disappearing because of gun-toting hunters and poisoned bait left by farmers.

▲ The Spanish eagle is another noble bird of prey threatened by farmers and hunters.

◄ The Komodo dragon is the world's largest living lizard—but it is under threat.

▼ The thylacine, or marsupial wolf, of Australia, has been hunted almost to extinction.

Animals under Threat

In the last century the great plains of North America swarmed with hundreds of millions of buffalo. Gross over-hunting has now reduced these great animals to a few carefully preserved herds.

A hundred years ago, only a few explorers had penetrated the vast expanses of the Brazilian rain forests. But this great jungle of unique animals and plants has now been invaded by human beings and their destructive machines, so that forest animals and plants are fast disappearing.

Of course, many kinds of animals and plants (in fact, *millions* of kinds) became extinct, or disappeared from the face of the Earth, long before human beings ever inhabited it. The dinosaurs, for example, ruled the Earth in vast numbers and variety for more than 150 million years, but despite their great and lasting success, they disappeared completely.

Today, it is the turn of the animals who succeeded the dinosaurs—the mammals, the birds, and the few remaining large reptiles—to come under threat of extinction. This threat comes mostly from people, who are now by far the most common large animal. As they change the Earth to suit themselves, they make it harder and harder for any other large animal, except domestic animals, to survive. We now realize that all wild animals are a valuable part of life, and try to conserve them. Many kinds of threatened animals are protected by law from being hunted and killed. Special wildlife reserves have also been set up.

Elephants in London Zoo.

Zoos

We see most wild animals in the zoo. When zoos first became popular, about a century ago, many kinds of animals could not be persuaded to breed and died after only a short while in captivity. With experience, zookeepers learned much more about the particular needs of wild animals. Today, animals in zoos live much longer and more of them are able to raise their young there. Some wild animals, though, still cannot survive easily in a zoo, which is why you will not usually find koala bears or platypuses there. Such delicate animals are often protected inside special nature reserves. Herds of much larger animals such as elephants and rhinos, are conserved inside game-parks or safari parks.

Predators

Tooth and Claw

▼ Although it is smaller than a lion or a tiger, the leopard is a mighty hunter. In fact, for its size it is the most powerful of all the great cats. Only a leopard has the strength to spring up into a tree holding prey as heavy as itself.

Hidden by leaves on a branch, a leopard waits to leap down onto the back of an unsuspecting forest gazelle. In the dusk an owl flits noiselessly over the meadows, its great eyes keeping a sharp lookout for signs of a mouse moving in the grass.

These are examples of solitary hunting animals, or predators, seeking their prey. But no animal can live entirely alone. Even lone predators are usually hunting for the whole family. They return with their catches to a nest or hideout where their hungry young are waiting.

Each kind of animal has its own way of defending itself from attack. Some are armed with sharp horns or lethal stings. Others can run so fast they cannot be caught. They may also rely on safety in numbers, and keep together in herds.

▲ Antelopes usually keep together in herds. A hunting animal will not attack a large group, but this antelope may have strayed too far away from the rest of the herd. Or it may have been too weak or sick to keep up as the herd ran from the prowling leopard.

and Prey

▼ Small but fierce—a Little Owl
returns to its nest in an English wood
with a large moth in its beak.

27

Hunters

Large predators may have to hunt over a very wide area to catch their prey. An eagle may soar over thousands of square miles during a week's hunting. A tiger will often scour as much as sixty miles of jungle pathways in search of a single meal.

Other big predators, however, may stay more or less in the same place, day after day, simply waiting for their prey to turn up. This is true of alligators and crocodiles, who often drag their prey into the water of their native rivers to drown it before eating it. Giant snakes such as boas and anacondas lie in wait for long periods for their prey. They are predators without being really active hunters.

Some predators, however, usually hunt in groups or families. Wolves and wild dogs hunt in packs. In lion families, lionesses normally do the hunting together. After the kill has been made the male lions often collect the first share and the best pickings.

In the oceans, killer whales are the most ferocious predators that hunt in family packs. They often attack great, harmless whales many times their own considerable size, tearing out the whales' huge tongues as the tastiest part of their bodies, before killing them. Yet these same killer whales, in captivity, are quite gentle with their human trainers.

▼ The golden eagle nests on high mountain ledges throughout the Northern Hemisphere. It is the largest bird of prey in the British Isles. It seizes its prey, such as hares and ptarmigan, in its long sharp talons.

Not all predators are large animals, of course. A weasel is a very small but extremely ferocious predator, which can kill a rabbit up to twenty times as heavy as itself, with a bite on the back of the neck. Spiders are perhaps the most familiar small predators, whether waiting in the center of a web for the arrival of insect prey, as in the case of the garden spider, or out actively hunting it, like the wolf spiders. The bird-eating spider of the tropical rain forests is much larger—about the same size as the small birds on which it preys. Piranha fishes are small, sharp-toothed predators which hunt in shoals and can soon strip a large animal to the bone.

Most feared of all hunters of the sea are the great killer sharks. Fast swimmers that hunt by scent, they can inflict terrible injuries on unwary seaside bathers, sometimes biting off whole limbs. Although many sharks may attack at once, they are not really pack animals. A shark is a solitary hunter that will attack anything that smells of blood—including any other wounded shark.

Defense and Disguise

Predatory animals do not have things all their own way. Their prey are not weak and defenseless. Most are well equipped to escape their attacker's hungry jaws, and healthy antelopes are fast enough to escape a hunting lion. A grown African buffalo is more than a match for any lion, and few predators will attack a porcupine.

These wild animals rely on speed, strength and armor (horns), and weapons (long, barbed quills) to defend themselves. But many other animals use defenses that are much less obvious—that are, in fact, disguises.

The best-known kind of disguise is camouflage. This is any type of coloring and patterning which makes the animal less visible against its background. The zebra's

▲ The porcupine fish normally has an average fish-shape, but when it is frightened or menaced it puffs itself up like this to become more difficult to swallow.

Some insect disguises: The green bush cricket (1) is camouflaged by color. The leaf insect (2), the stick insect (3), the thorn-tree hopper (4) and the leaf butterfly (5), as their names suggest, match their surroundings perfectly. By contrast the wasp (6), the cinnabar moth (7) and the puss moth caterpillar (8) use bright colors to warn predators to keep away.

T. BOYER

▲ With its armory of long, sharp, barbed quills, a porcupine is safe from attack— even from lions, unless they are very hungry indeed.

The brilliant colors of this little South American tree frog warn of its extreme poisonousness. Its only enemies are forest Indians, who capture and kill it for its deadly poison, which they will then use to tip their arrows. One scratch from such an arrow will bring a monkey toppling down from a tree.

▲ Predators as well as prey use camouflage to remain unseen. Although this tiger is visible enough in the open, its stripes will conceal it in longer grass.

stripes and the giraffe's brown and white pattern make them harder to see in the African trees and grasses. Many insects, such as greenfly, grasshoppers and crickets, are green, and so are hard to see among green leaves and grass. Other insects are shaped as well as colored to resemble the plant on which they live. If the leaf insect, stick insect, thorn-tree hopper and leaf butterfly were not numbered in the diagram, they would be very difficult to spot.

Instead of disguising themselves, some prey animals, such as the wasp and cinnabar moth, look as visible as possible by means of bright, staring colors, usually yellow, black and red. These colors warn a predator that the animal stings or tastes nasty, and the predator learns to leave it alone. The puss moth can in addition squirt a pungent liquid at any enemy rash enough to attack it.

Even "cleverer" prey animals come to resemble these nasty-tasting species, so that predators leave them alone too, even though they don't taste nasty or sting. A hoverfly, for example, looks very like a wasp.

Scavengers

Nothing is wasted in the wild. After a large predator, such as a lion or tiger, has made its kill and eaten its fill, perhaps only some skin and bone remains of its prey. But even this will soon disappear after the scavengers have been to work.

These are the tidiers-up of nature. Not only do they remove bits of animals that have been killed as prey, but they also eat and dispose of the bodies of creatures who have died of disease, or old age, or as the result of a fall or other accident. Some scavengers specialize in removing and eating the dung that larger animals drop.

Scavenging may seem an unpleasant way of life. Obviously the scavengers themselves do not think so—a bit of really smelly carrion appeals to a scavenger as a really tasty meal. And scavenging is vital. Just think of what would happen if all the skin and bones, all the dead bodies, and all the dung in nature just lay around and piled up!

At one time, it was thought that the hyena, a large meat-eater, lived entirely by scavenging. Its jaws are powerful enough to crack the thickest and strongest bones left behind by the lion. But now we know that the hyena often makes its own kills—which the lion is not averse to scavenging.

Not all scavengers are large. Jackals, foxes and vultures are medium-sized animals. Others are small. These include many little fishes (the oceans need tidying up too) and the dung beetles pictured on these pages.

But the most important scavengers of all are much too small to be seen without a microscope. These are the bacteria and fungi that cause decay, and so return all once-living things back to the soil to provide plants with their vital mineral food.

◄ The spotted hyena is a large scavenger which eats carrion and even dung. But it also preys on zebras and antelopes.

► These scarab beetles are scavenging dung, which they form into a ball to roll away to their nest as food for their grubs.

◄ On this large carcass lying on the hot African grasslands are perched two types of medium-sized scavengers—vultures and ravens. What little they leave will be finished off by beetles and other very small scavengers.

▼ The marabou is a rather ugly stork that specializes in scavenging.

◄ The fox once hunted only in the countryside but has now become a town scavenger. Being an intelligent animal, it knows what can be gotten from overfull garbage cans!

Living Together

The Nile crocodile is the greatest and most ferocious of living reptiles, yet it allows these small birds to roam about its body and even inside its fearsomely toothed jaws. The reason is that the birds eat parasites and dead skin, so helping both themselves and the crocodile. This is a form of symbiosis.

Baboon Family Life

Baboons are monkeys that live mostly on the ground, in large families or troops. They lead a very definite family life in which everyone has his or her special position and duties. These are shown in the picture by colors. The large adult male baboons, shown pale blue, are the guardians and fathers of the troop. They defend the troop against enemies. One adult male usually acts as lookout when the troop is feeding, and barks a warning if a fast escape is necessary. Each adult male has several mates, shown light brown. These may have one, or unusually two, small baby baboons clinging to them, shown red. Older juveniles, dark blue, often leave their mothers to play in groups. Adolescents, shown dark brown, help forage for food and keep a lookout.

Grooming is important in keeping the troop together. One of these females is grooming her husband, but all ranks except the small babies will groom other troop members. Grooming is both comforting and cleaning.

Symbiosis

Symbiosis is the closest kind of living together. Neither partner in the symbiosis can live easily, or at all, without the other. To take the example of the crocodile and the cleaner-birds shown on the left: without the crocodile the birds could not get their food, and without the cleaner-birds the crocodile's skin would soon become infested with parasites.

Other symbiotic partnerships may be even closer. Small insects called termites live in large colonies and often eat wood. But they are unable to digest this without microscopic, one-celled protozoa which live inside their bodies. Neither termite nor protozoa can live without the other. But protozoa which live inside animals can also cause disease— for example, malaria. Many helpful symbionts have turned into harmful parasites, and *vice versa*.

This cuckoo, being fed by its host or foster parent, a dunnock, is a parasite. As an egg it was laid in the foster parents' nest. Now it is the only chick remaining alive, and is much bigger than the host birds that have to feed it. This is very unusual among parasites, which are nearly all much smaller than their hosts.

Some animals are hunters while others are hunted. But mainly, wild animals live together in nature. Even predators and their prey, such as the lions, zebras and antelopes on the African plains, live peaceably together for most of the time. Except at hunting time, they take little notice of one another.

Some animals live very close together, in families. Such are the lions and the monkey families, including the baboon troop described on these pages. Family life is more complicated than herd life, and family animals are generally more intelligent than herd animals.

Different kinds of animals may depend upon one another for a living or a useful service. One example of this is the crocodile and cleaner-birds shown in the picture. Or, one animal may be a harmful parasite of another, as the cuckoo is of the dunnock and many other small birds.

Animals and Plants

All animal life depends, finally, on plant life. This fox feeds on the rabbit and the rabbit feeds on the green plant. But the green plant, to build up its own body, needs only mineral salts and water from the soil, carbon dioxide from the air, and energy from the Sun.

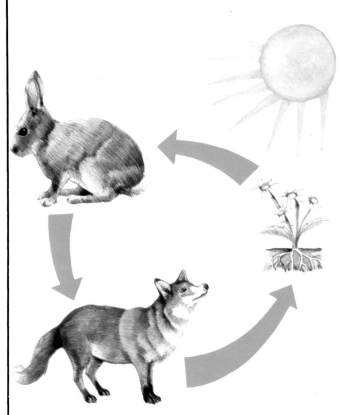

▶ A red-deer doe nibbles at tree leaves. This kind of plant-eating is called browsing, whereas nibbling grass and other ground plants is called grazing.

You usually find most animals where there are most plants. For example, a patch of grassland or jungle contains more wild animals than the same area of desert or high mountain.

As shown in the diagram above, green plants are what make animal life possible. This is so even in the oceans, where very few green plants, except a few floating seaweeds, are to be seen. The vast majority of oceanic plants are very tiny, often consisting of only a single living cell. These are the green plants of the plankton, the almost invisible floating life of the oceans. Larger oceanic animals feed on the tiny plankton, plants and animals. Still larger animals eat *them*, and so on. This is called a food chain.

Food chains also occur in life on land. The diagram shows a simple food chain: plant-rabbit-fox. A rather longer food chain is plant-beetle-bird-wild cat. There are many others.

Index

Acknowledgements

Cover Pat Morris *center;* Endpapers Pat Morris; 8 NHPA/Philip Wayre; 10 NHPA/K.H. Switak; 13 SATOUR; 14 Zefa; 17 Pat Morris; 19 NHPA; 22 C. R. Roberts *top,* Zefa *bottom;* 23 Pat Morris *top* and *center;* 26 Zoological Society of London/ Michael Lyster; 27 NHPA; 28 NHPA; 29 Seaphot; 30 Seaphot/Christian Petron; 31 Zoological Society of London *top,* NHPA *bottom;* 32 Pat Morris, 32/3 NHPA; 33 Pat Morris *center,* NHPA *bottom;* 35 NHPA; 36 Zefa.

Picture research: Penny Warn.